Study Guide
Jennifer Adams Aldrich

Introduction to Hospitality

THIRD EDITION

John R. Walker, D.B.A., FMP.
Marshall Professor and Director
Hotel, Restaurant, and Tourism Management
Alliant International University
San Diego, California

Upper Saddle River, New Jersey 07458

Copyright © 2002 by Pearson Education, Inc., Upper Saddle River, New Jersey 07458. All rights reserved. Printed in the United States of America. This publication is protected by Copyright and permission should be obtained from the publisher prior to any prohibited reproduction, storage in a retrieval system, or transmission in any form or by any means, electronic, mechanical, photocopying, recording, or likewise. For Information regarding permission(s), write to: Rights and Permissions Department.

10 9 8 7 6 5 4 3 2 1
ISBN 0-13-061361-4

Contents

Chapter One	Introduction	1
Chapter Two	Tourism	8
Chapter Three	The Hotel Business: Development and Classification	16
Chapter Four	Hotel and Rooms Division Operation	23
Chapter Five	Hotel Operations: Food and Beverage Division	31
Chapter Six	The Culinary Arts and Restaurant Business: Development and Classification	39
Chapter Seven	Restaurant Operations	46
Chapter Eight	Managed Services	54
Chapter Nine	Beverages	61
Chapter Ten	Recreation and Leisure	68
Chapter Eleven	The Gaming Entertainment Industry	74
Chapter Twelve	Meetings, Conventions, and Expositions	79
Chapter Thirteen	Marketing, Human Resources, and Culture	86
Chapter Fourteen	Leadership and Management	94
Answer Key		102

Preface

The hospitality industry is an incredibly exciting and diverse field. Congratulations on taking your first steps toward a professional career in this rewarding and challenging industry!

This Study Guide has been developed to help you make the most of your study time and to serve a resource for the future. By completing the study guide _after_ you have thoroughly read the text, you will enrich your understanding of important concepts. A separate workbook section has been developed for each chapter of the text and contains the following elements:

- Key Words and Concepts
- Chapter Reflection
- Study Questions

Best wishes for success in your career, and please feel free to e-mail me with your comments on this study guide at jaldrich@jwu.edu.

Chapter One: Introduction

After reading and studying Chapter One, you should be able to do the following:
1. Name the characteristics of the hospitality industry.
2. Explain corporate philosophy as we enter the twenty-first century.
3. Discuss why service has become such as important facet of the hospitality industry.
4. Understand how internships, mentoring, and job shadowing aids those who choose the hospitality industry as a career path.
5. Write a résumé.
6. Prepare for a job interview.

The following exercises have been designed to enhance your understanding of the chapter and to assist your studying. These exercises will be most effective if attempted **after** reading the chapter. In addition, space has been provided for you to add terms, notes, and concepts that your instructor may have introduced.

I. Key Words and Concepts

Key Word or Concept	Explanation
1. Average daily rate (ADR)	
2. Back-of-the-house	
3. Corporate culture	
4. Corporate philosophy	
5. Front-of-the-house	
6. Goal	
7. Graveyard shift	
8. Guest satisfaction	
9. Hospitality	
10. Inseparability	
11. Intangible	
12. Internships	
13. Job shadowing	
14. Leadership	

15. Mentor	
16.	
17.	
18.	
19.	
20.	

II. Chapter Reflection

1. For each of the persons or corporations listed in the following section, briefly describe the major contributions (described in this chapter), that they have made which have impacted the development of the hospitality industry.

J.W. Marriott:

Jan Carlson:

The Ritz Carlton Hotel Company:

The Disney Corporation:

2. What are the major segments of the hospitality and tourism industries? How do the segments relate to each other?

3. List the benefits that hospitality companies can realize as a result of embracing the Total Quality Management (TQM) process.

4. List several characteristics that Leaders must possess in order to be successful.

III. Study Questions

Fill in the Blanks

1. The _____ has enjoyed a rich history as a symbol of welcome, friendship, and hospitality.

2. The _____ industry is largest and fastest growing industry in the world.

3. Examples of the _____ segment of the hospitality industry include airlines, military facilities, schools, colleges, and business and industry.

4. Effective leaders are those who make things happen because they have developed the _____, _____, and _____ necessary to get the job done.

5. The _____ is the highest level of national recognition for quality in the United States. It was earned by the _____ Hotel company in 1993 and 1999.

6. A _____ refers to any number of interactions with staff that give guests an impression of the overall quality of service within an operation.

7. According to the motto of the Ritz-Carlton Hotel Company, their employees are _____ serving _____.

8. Disney uses a team approach to interviewing called _____ as a means of determining how well the prospective employees will be able to _____.

9. _____ provide students with an excellent opportunity to learn about a particular company.

10. Recruiters typically look to three things when judging a student's qualifications for a position: _____, _____, and _____.

11. A _____ should always be written to an interviewer after a job interview.

12. List the three important steps that managers should follow when trying to implement change.

_____

_____

_____

True/False

1. _____ Evenings and weekends are included in the normal workweek in the hospitality industry.

2. _____ Total Quality Management (TQM) is a continuous process.

3. _____ TQM focuses on error detection, while Quality Control (QC) focuses on error prevention.

4. _____ If you do not like the assignment you have been given while while working on an internship, be sure to complain about it being grunt work.

5. _____ A mentor can help you avoid some basic career mistakes by offering advice.

6. _____ Extracurricular activities should never be discussed on a résumé.

7. _____ Asking any questions during a job interview shows the interviewer that you have not prepared for the interview.

8. _____ The hospitality industry is in the business of giving service.

Matching

1. _____ Corporate culture   a) a short statement of central purposes, strategies, and values of a company

2. _____ Objective   b) the overall style or feel of a company

3. _____ Goal   c) a quantification of a goal in measurable terms

4. _____ Strategies/ tactics   d) a broad statement of what a company or department wishes to accomplish

5. _____ Mission statement   e) actions needed to accomplish a goal

Short Answer

1. Define the following terms and explain how they relate to the hospitality industry: a) *intangibility,* b) *inseparability,* c) *perishibility.*

_____
_____
_____
_____

2. Review the "7 Deadly Sins of Service" and discuss how they might be avoided by workers in the hospitality industry.

_____
_____
_____
_____

3. Explain the difference between an "Internal Customer" and an "External Customer."

___

4. List five of the important steps that should be followed when preparing for a job interview, and explain why they are important.

___

Chapter Two: Tourism

After reading and studying Chapter Two, you should be able to do the following:
1. Define tourism.
2. Trace the five epochs (or periods) of tourism.
3. Describe the evolution of the major travel modes.
4. Outline the important international and domestic tourism organizations.
5. Describe the economic impact of tourism.
6. Identify promoters of tourism.
7. List reasons why people travel.
8. Describe the sociocultural impact of tourism.
9. Describe ecotourism.

The following exercises have been designed to enhance your understanding of the chapter and to assist your studying. These exercises will be most effective if attempted **after** reading the chapter. In addition, space has been provided for you to add terms, notes, and concepts that your instructor may have introduced.

I. Key Words and Concepts

Key Word or Concept	Explanation
1. Agenda 21	
2. The Bermuda Agreement	
3. Commission caps	
4. Corporate travel manager	
5. Destination management company	
6. Eco-tourism	
7. Hub and Spoke System	
8. Multiplier effect	
9. Pleasure travel	
10. Sustainable tourism	
11. Ticketless travel	
12. Tour operators	
13. Tourist	

14. Travel agents	
15. Travel and tour wholesalers	
16.	
17.	
18.	
19.	
20.	

II. Chapter Reflection

1. The Tourism industry is broad in its scope. In your own words, identify the major segments of the tourism industry and how they impact the world economy.

2. Define the term "tourist."

3. Chapter Two details the development of the tourism industry through five major epochs or periods. Identify the five epochs, the major catalyst for change, and how the hospitality industry adapted to meet the changing needs of travelers.

4. There are many international and domestic organizations that serve to develop, regulate, and promote tourism. In the spaces provided below, list the organizations involved and their particular role in the tourism industry.

International Organizations

Domestic Organizations

5. Describe the services provided by Travel Agents.

III. Study Questions

Fill in the Blanks

1. The Roman Empire maintained a road system that ranged from _____ to _____.

2. _____ was created by the U.S. government to prevent the collapse of the passenger rail system.

3. _____, _____, _____, and _____ are four major effects of airline deregulation.

4. _____ have been established by many cities to attract and retain visitors to the city.

5. _____ is the professional certification available to Travel Agents through ICTA.

6. List the three reasons that cruise ships sail under foreign flags.

   a) _____
   b) _____
   c) _____

7. Name three types of Travel Tourism wholesalers.

    a)_____

    b)_____

    c)_____

8. Name the four basic considerations that influence travel (McIntosh and Goeldner).

    a)_____

    b)_____

    c)_____

    d)_____

True/False

1. _____ Tourism is the world's largest industry.

2. _____ Hub and Spoke systems have contributed to airline financial losses.

3. _____ Transient occupancy tax (TOT) provides much of the funding for CVBs.

4. _____ The term "leakage" refers to the predictable decline in tourism which occurs when a destination becomes "mainstream."

5. _____ A travel agent serves as broker between the client and the travel service provider.

6. _____ The vast majority of travel is business related.

7. _____ Interpersonal motivation for travel includes the desire for recognition and a good reputation.

8. _____ Psychocentrics prefer familiar travel destinations, whereas allocentrics prefer new and different destinations.

9. _____ Sales of airline tickets over the Internet have decreased commissions received by travel agents.

10. _____ Business travelers contribute more than other travelers to airlines' earnings.

11. _____ Ecotourism is the fastest growing segment of the tourism industry.

12. _____ A person's culturally based expectations can influence his or her level of satisfaction with a travel experience.

Matching

1. _____ World Tourism Organization (WTO) a) represents 34 countries in Asia

2. _____ International Civil Aviation Organization (ICAO) b) leads money for tourism development

3. _____ International Air Transportation Association (IATA) c) assists countries with various development projects

4. _____ World Bank (WB) d) created in 1981 by the National Tourism Policy Act

5. _____ U.S. Travel and Tourism Administration (USTTA) e) global organization that regulates most international airlines

6. _____ Travel Industry of America (TIA) f) contributes to the sound economic development in member and non-member countries

7. _____ United Nations Development Program (UNDP) g) coordinates the development of all civil aviation

8. _____ Pacific Area Travel Association (PATA) h) represents the common interests of the U.S. travel industry

9. _____ Organization for Economic Cooperation and Development i) most widely recognized tourism organization in the world

Short Answer

1. Name the major elements of the Bermuda Agreement and detail the importance of this agreement.

2. Describe amenities common to many cruise ships. Define the following cruise market segments -- mass market, middle market, and luxury market.

3. Detail the impact of on-line services upon the travel services industry.

4. Explain the reasons why travel is expected to increase in the coming years.

_____

_____

_____

_____

_____

5. Identify the positive and negative sociocutural influences that tourism can create.

_____

_____

_____

_____

_____

6. Detail the world-wide economic impact of tourism.

_____

_____

_____

_____

_____

Chapter Three:
The Hotel Business: Development and Classification

After reading and studying Chapter Three, you should be able to do the following:

1. Describe briefly the development of the US lodging industry.
2. Define the following terms: *hotel franchising, partnerships, leasing, syndicates and management contracts.*
3. Discuss financial aspects of hotel development.
4. Classify hotels by type, location, and price.
5. Explain vertical integration.
6. Name some prestigious and unusual hotels.
7. Describe the effects of a global economy on the hotel industry.

The following exercises have been designed to enhance your understanding of the chapter and to assist your studying. These exercises will be most effective if attempted **after** reading the chapter. In addition, space has been provided for you to add terms, notes, and concepts that your instructor may have introduced.

I. Key Words and Concepts

Key Word or Concept	Explanation
1. Creative financing	
2. Bed and Breakfast Inns	
3. All-Suite extended stay hotels	
4. Economic downturn	
5. Franchising	
6. Globalization	
7. Inflation	
8. Interest rates	
9. Leasing	
10. Leasing agreements	
11. Marketing consortium	
12. Management contracts	
13. Midprice range	
14. Partnership	

15. Portfolio Financing	
16. REIT	
17. Syndicates	
18. Vacation Ownership	
19.	
20.	
21.	
22.	

II. Chapter Reflection

1. Explain hotel development in the United States. Include examples to document each major phase, from colonial times to the present.

2. Identify and explain the different methods of hotel classification.

3. Define vacation ownership and detail the reasons why this segment of the industry has been gaining in popularity.

4. Identify factors that should be considered before buying a franchise.

III. Study Questions

Fill in the Blanks

1. _____ substantially changed the nature of the hotel industry.

2. _____ spurred the growth of new hotels and motels during the 1940s, 1950s, and 1960s.

3. The average franchise agreement requires a payment of _____ to _____ of room revenue to the franchisor.

4. The hospitality industry is considered to have a high degree of risk because of these two major factors: _____ and _____.

5. _____ and _____ are the only REIT's that are allowed to both manage and own hotel properties.

6. _____ are the most common form of real estate financing for hotels.

7. Guests of remote resort properties are sometimes referred to as _____ clientele because they may spend their entire stay on the property.

True/False

1. _____ Vertical integration refers to the practice of hotel companies purchasing related companies such as airlines or travel agencies.

2. _____ Marketing consortiums are comprised of independent hotel properties that refer business to each other.

3. _____ The Four Seasons Hotel chain has the distinction of being the only hospitality company that has earned the Malcolm Baldrige National Quality Award.

4. _____ A capsule hotel is a budget hotel property built with modular units.

5. _____ In order to earn a reasonable return on investment, a hotel must charge $1 in room rate for every $1,000 spent to purchase or construct the property.

6. _____ In signing a franchise agreement, the franchisee agrees to maintain certain standards and practices required by the franshisor.

7. _____ Current financing conditions are very favorable for hotel development.

8. _____ Room rates charged by Bed and Breakfast operations are often appealing to price sensitive travelers.

9. _____ The United States has no formal hotel classification system.

10. _____ Hotel development can be an important stabilizing factor in developing countries.

Matching

1. _____ Airport Hotels   a) offer a broad range of services, business feature; often luxurious

2. _____ Casino Hotels   b) average 200 to 600 rooms; cater to business travelers

3. _____ Full Service Hotels   c) clean, reasonably priced, without full service frills

4. _____ Freeway Hotels and Motels   d) cater primarily to business, professional/technical, and relocating families

5. _____ Extended-Stay Hotels   e) an alternative lodging experience; often owner occupied

6. _____ Economy/ Budget Hotels   f) provide facilities for groups attending and holding meetings

7. _____ Bed and Breakfast Inns   g) are a significant segment of the entertainment industry and are becoming increasingly family friendly

8. _____ All-Suite, Extended-Stay Hotels   h) came into prominence in the 1950s and 1960s

9. _____ Convention Hotels   i) provide large rooms that often include lounge and kitchenette areas

Short Answer

1. Discuss the advantages and disadvantages of the franchise agreement from the perspective of the franchisor and the franchisee.

2. List the reasons that people construct hotels.

3. Identify the necessary groundwork to achieve a favorable financing package for hotel development.

4. What steps have resorts hotels taken to increase business and better serve the needs of guests?

_____

_____

_____

_____

_____

_____

Chapter Four: Hotel and Rooms Division Operation

After reading and studying Chapter Four, you should be able to do the following:

1. Outline the duties and responsibilities of key executives and department heads.
2. Draw an organizational chart of the rooms division of a hotel and identify the executive committee members.
3. Describe the main functions of the rooms division, front desk, and night audit.
4. Describe property management systems and discuss yield management.
5. Calculate occupancy percentages, average daily rates, and actual percentage of potential rooms revenues.
6. Outline the importance of the reservations and guest service functions.
7. List the complexities and challenges of the concierge, housekeeping, and security/loss prevention departments.

The following exercises have been designed to enhance your understanding of the chapter and to assist your studying. These exercises will be most effective if attempted **after** reading the chapter. In addition, space has been provided for you to add terms, notes, and concepts that your instructor may have introduced.

I. Key Words and Concepts

Key Word or Concept	Explanation
1. Accounting Director	
2. Average daily rate (ADR)	
3. Catastrophe Plan	
4. CBX/ PBX	
5. Central reservations system	
6. Chief accountant/ controller	
7. City ledger	
8. Confirmed reservation	
9. Guaranteed reservation	
10. Daily report	
11. Engineering Director	
12. Executive committee	
13. Food and Beverage Director	

14. Guest Service Director	
15. Housekeeping	
16. Human Resources Director	
17. Inventory control	
18. Marketing and Sales Director	
19. Property management systems	
20. Reservation Department	
21. Rev par	
22. Room occupancy percentage	
23. Room rates	
24. Security/ loss prevention	
25. Yield management	
26.	
27.	
28.	

II. Chapter Reflection

1. Summarize the roles and responsibilities of the following hotel staff:
   a) Hotel General Manager
   b) Rooms Division Manager
   c) Front Office Manager
   d) Night Auditor
   e) Reservations Manager
   f) Concierge
   g) Executive Housekeeper
   h) Desk Clerk

2. Identify the personal qualities that are important to successful General Managers and explain how these qualities contribute to the performance of the property.

3. What are the main duties of the front office morning shift? What are the main duties of the front office evening shift? What information must be shared between shifts?

4. Formula Summary

ADR =

ROP =

Rate Achievement Factor =

Yield Percentage =

RevPar =

% of Potential Rooms Revenue =

III. Study Questions

Fill in the Blanks

1. The primary function of a hotel is to _____.

2. Hotels exist to _____ and to _____.

3. Two methods used to increase the average daily rate (ADR) are _____ and _____.

4. Yield management requires that hotels balance _____ and

_____ in order to maximize revenues.

5. The _____ is a special account for companies that have established credit with the hotel.

6. The Hotel Industry Switch Company (THISCO) created a way to share rooms availability information between _____ and _____.

7. The abbreviation PABS stands for _____ _____ which is an important element of yield management.

8. Productivity in the housekeeper department is measured by _____ _____.

9. List the three major responsibilities of Hotel General Managers.
   a) _____
   b) _____
   c) _____

10. Property management systems (PMS) provide software packages to assist with the following front office functions:
    a) _____
    b) _____
    c) _____
    d) _____

True/ False

1. _____ Hotels are comprised of several revenue and cost centers.

2. _____ General Managers should never hire department heads who know more about a particular area then they do.

3. _____ General Managers should allow the cultural traditions of guests and employees to influence the management of the hotel property.

4. _____ The communications center is not a revenue center for the hotel.

5. _____ The reservations department is the largest department within the hotel.

6. _____ Housekeeping associates clean and service an average of 35 to 40 rooms per day.

7. _____ The Employee Right to Know Act requires employers to notify employees about the dangers of chemicals they work with.

8. _____ Electronic key systems are less secure than traditional key systems.

9. _____ The front desk closes briefly between 12:00AM and 2:00AM, to allow the Night Audit staff to balance guest accounts.

10. _____ Cleanliness is a key consideration for guests when making room reservations.

Matching

1. _____ VR   a) Room is undergoing redecoration or maintenance. Room is not available for sale.

2. _____ OC   b) A personal inspection is required to determine if room is occupied or vacant.

3. _____ DND   c) The room is unoccupied and is clean. It is ready for sale.

4. _____ OD   d) The room is occupied and daily cleaning has occurred. Room is not available for sale.

5. _____ OO   e) The room is occupied and daily cleaning has occurred. However, additional inspection and/or maintenance is needed. Room is not available for sale.

6. _____ V/O   f) The room is occupied, but daily cleaning has not yet occurred. Room is not available for sale.

7. _____ OR   g) The room is occupied, but daily cleaning has not yet occurred, because a "Do not Disturb" sign has been placed on the door.

Short Answer

1. Discuss the role of the Executive Committee in the management of a hotel property.

2. List the typical sources of reservations inquires.

3. Describe the typical process involved in making a reservation from the hotel's perspective. Discuss the different types of reservations that may be made.

4. What obligations do hotels have to their guests with regard to safety and security? What elements must be included in a comprehensive security plan?

Chapter Five: Hotel Operations: Food and Beverage Division

After reading and studying Chapter Five, you should be able to do the following:

1. Describe the duties and responsibilities of a food and beverage director and other key departments.
2. Describe a typical food and beverage director's day.
3. State the functions and responsibilities of the food and beverage departments.
4. Perform computations using key food and beverage operating ratios.

The following exercises have been designed to enhance your understanding of the chapter and to assist your studying. These exercises will be most effective if attempted **after** reading the chapter. In addition, space has been provided for you to add terms, notes, and concepts that your instructor may have introduced.

I. Key Words and Concepts

Key Word or Concept	Explanation
1. Banquet	
2. Banquet Event Order (BEO)	
3. Brigade	
4. Capture rate	
5. Catering	
6. Chef de partie	
7. Chef tournant	
8. Contribution margin	
9. Lounges/ bars	
10. Perpetual inventory	
11. Pilferage	
12. Pour/cost percentage	
13. Ratios	
14. Shopper	
15. Sommelier	
16. Sous Chef	

17. Sous-vide	
18.	
19.	
20.	
21.	
22.	

II. Chapter Reflection

1. Summarize the roles and responsibilities of the following hotel staff:
    a) Food and Beverage Director
    b) Executive Chef / Kitchen Manager
    c) Chief Steward
    d) Catering Director
    e) Catering Service Manager
    f) Restaurant Manager
    g) Catering Coordinator

2. Identify the different types of food and beverage outlets typically found within full service hotel properties.

3. Identify the technical and leadership skills necessary to be successful in the position of Director of Catering.

4. Detail, in chronological order, the steps involved in booking a function.

5. Formula Summary

Contribution Margin =

Covers per person hour =

Food Cost Percentage =

Labor Cost Percentage =

Pour Cost =

III. Study Questions

Fill in the Blanks

1. The Director of Food and Beverage reports to the _____.

2. Approximately _____ of a hotel's operating profit comes from food and beverage operations.

3. The monthly forecast for the food and beverage department is completed between the _____ and _____ of each month.

4. Financial results in the food and beverage department are generally expressed as _____.

5. Most hotel kitchens are organized using the _____ system which was developed by _____.

6. Bar staff are expected to maintain a standard pour cost of _____ to _____.

7. Maintenance of inventory, back of the house cleanliness, and pest control management are the responsibilities of the _____.

8. A _____ refers to a group of people who eat together at one time, whereas _____ refers to variety of occasions when people may eat at varying times.

9. The purpose of the _____ or _____ is to inform the client and hotel personnel about an upcoming function taking place at the hotel.

10. Guests order room service in two main ways, by _____ and _____.

11. List the five most frequent catering events that take place in hotels.
    a)_____
    b)_____
    c)_____
    d)_____
    e)_____

12. List four ways that hotels have sought to increase efficiency in the room service operations.

   a)_____

   b)_____

   c)_____

   d)_____

True/ False

1. _____ Room service menus should feature only the finest gourmet cuisine.

2. _____ Most hotels have eliminated in-room dining as a cost saving measure.

3. _____ Another term for the function diary is the "bible."

4. _____ The guaranteed number of guest to attend a catered function is normally required about three weeks before the event.

5. _____ The Executive Chef has final approval of all catering menus.

6. _____ The profit percentage earned on beverages is higher than that earned on food items.

7. _____ The term capture rate refers the number of in-house guests that dine in the hotel's food and beverage outlets.

8. _____ Rightsizing refers to the practice of hiring highly skilled employees.

9. _____ Annual forecast for the food and beverage department are usually completed between the months of January and March.

10. _____ All-suite properties generally achieve a 7% food and beverage profit percentage because of the complimentary meals and beverages provided to guests.

Matching

1. _____ Theater style a) preferred when interaction between attendees in desired; commonly used for training sessions and workshops

2. _____ Classroom style b) room is usually set with round tables with seating for 8 to 10 guests per table

3. _____ Horseshoe style c) room is set with rows of chairs and two or more aisles; preferred when audio visual equipment will be used

4. _____ Dinner style d) provides guests with a writing surface; costly to set and breakdown

Short Answer

1. Describe the typical day of a hotel's Food and Beverage Director.

2. Explain the efforts made by hotels to increase the number of guests who dine in their on-property food and beverage outlets.

3. Identify the ways employees can pilfer from bar operations and explain what steps managers can take to control these problems.

4. List and describe the different types of bars found within large hotels.

5. Detail the main sources of business leads for the Catering Sales Department.

Chapter Six:
The Culinary Arts and Restaurant Business: Development and Classification

After reading and studying Chapter Six, you should be able to do the following:

1. Describe the history and evolution of culinary arts.
2. Know the food-safety suggestions.
3. Trace the history and development of the restaurant business.
4. List the factors that influence restaurant concept and marketing.
5. Discuss the important elements in menu planning.
6. Outline the development of a restaurant chain.
7. Describe the different characteristics of chain and independent restaurants.
8. Identify some of the top chain and independent restaurants.
9. List classifications of restaurants

The following exercises have been designed to enhance your understanding of the chapter and to assist your studying. These exercises will be most effective if attempted **after** reading the chapter. In addition, space has been provided for you to add terms, notes, and concepts that your instructor may have introduced.

I. Key Words and Concepts

Key Word or Concept	Explanation
1. Actual market share	
2. Ambiance	
3. Atmosphere	
4. Catchment area	
5. Chain restaurants	
6. Contribution margin	
7. Culinary arts	
8. Fair market share	
9. Food cost percentage	
10. Haute cuisine	

11. Independent restaurants	
12. Infusion	
13. Menu planning	
14. Mother sauce	
15. Niche	
16. Nouvelle cuisine	
17. Puree	
18. Roux	
19. Sales volume	
20. Weighted average	
21.	
22.	
23.	
24.	

II. Chapter Reflection

1. Outline the significant historical developments that have influenced the field of culinary arts.

2. Explain the reasons why people dine out in restaurants.

| |
| |
| |
| |
| |
| |
| |
| |

3. Author an original definition for each of the following types of restaurant operations:
   a) Casual dining   f) Family restaurant
   b) Casual up-scale   g) Fine dining
   c) Celebrity owned   h) Quick service
   d) Ethnic   i) Specialty
   e) Theme   j) Dinner house

| |
| |
| |
| |
| |
| |
| |
| |
| |
| |
| |
| |
| |
| |
| |
| |

4. Define the criteria that should be considered when selecting a restaurant location.

5. List the considerations that impact menu development.

III. Study Questions

Fill in the Blanks

1. A _____ is a marketing term used to describe a share of a restaurant market.

2. The _____ is the area surrounding a restaurant, from which the restaurant is likely to draw the majority of their customers.

3. The average number of people per restaurants in the U.S. is _____.

4. Menus usually have _____ appetizers, _____ soups, a few salads, _____ entrees, and _____ desserts.

5. _____ and _____ have a direct impact on how efficiently food can be produced by the kitchen staff.

6. _____ are noted as having especially efficient kitchen operations.

7. _____ and _____ are the two principal methods of menu pricing.

8. The "weighted average" method of menu pricing considers three factors -- _____, _____, and _____.

9. _____ require restaurants to make truthful statements in menu descriptions.

10. Chicken restaurants remain popular because it is cheap to produce, _____, and _____.

11. Steak restaurants attract primarily _____ and _____ diners.

12. What are the six major types of menus?

    a) _____
    b) _____
    c) _____
    d) _____
    e) _____
    f) _____

13. List four practices utilized in "Back to Basic Cooking."

    a) _____
    b) _____
    c) _____
    d) _____

True/False

1. _____ Theme restaurants seek to impress guests with extensive menus.

2. _____ Sandwich shops are the fastest growing type of specialty restaurants in the U.S.

3. _____ The fifteen mother sauces are considered to be the foundation of classical French cooking.

4. _____ Seafood restaurants have changed food preparation techniques in response to consumer health concerns.

5. _____ As the number of meals consumed away from home increases, so does the risk of food-borne illness.

6. _____ Quick Service Restaurants are attempting to increase flat sales through co-branding.

7. _____ A menu is designed to be both a sales tools and a motivational device.

8. _____ Mother's Day is the most popular day for dining out.

9. _____ Signature items should be placed at the menu focal point.

10. _____ Most experts agree that there are two main categories of restaurants - full service and quick service.

Short Answer

1. Explain the reasons why McDonald's Restaurants have been so successful.

_____
_____
_____
_____
_____
_____

2. What are the reasons why a successful full-service national restaurant chain has not been established?

3. Identify and explain the factors that should be considered when establishing the price to be charged for menu items.

4. Review the food safety suggestions discussed in the chapter. Explain how a manager should help his or her employees to understand the importance of these practices and ensure employee compliance.

Chapter Seven: Restaurant Operations

After reading and studying Chapter Seven, you should be able to do the following:

1. Apply the forecasting technique used in the chapter to measure expected volume of business.
2. Name and describe the various types of service.
3. Explain the important aspects of food production.
4. Describe the key points in purchasing, receiving, storing, and issuing.
5. Explain the differences between controllable expenses and fixed costs.
6. Explain the components of an income statement and operating ratios.
7. Describe the important aspects of control systems for a restaurant operation.
8. Outline the functional areas and tasks of a food service/restaurant manager.

The following exercises have been designed to enhance your understanding of the chapter and to assist your studying. These exercises will be most effective if attempted **after** reading the chapter. In addition, space has been provided for you to add terms, notes, and concepts that your instructor may have introduced.

I. Key Words and Concepts

Key Word or Concept	Explanation
1. Average guest check	
2. Back of the house	
3. Balance sheet profits	
4. Beverage cost percentage	
5. Budgeting	
6. Cooking line	
7. Control	
8. Controllable expenses	
9. First-In, First-Out (FIFO)	
10. Curbside appeal	
11. Employee recognition	
12. Fixed costs	
13. Front of the house	

14. Gross profit	
15. Guest counts on covers	
16. Haute Cuisine	
17. Income statement	
18. Kitchen layout	
19. Kitchen manager	
20. Net profit	
21. Operating ratios	
22. Par stock	
23. Prime cost	
24. Product specification	
25. Production control sheets	
26. Purchase order	
27. Purchasing	
28. Receiving	
29. Restaurant forecasting	
30. Uniform system of accounts	
31. Variable cost	
32.	
33.	
34.	

II. Chapter Reflection

1. Summarize the roles and responsibilities of the following restaurant staff:
   a) Chef de rang
   b) Commis de rang
   c) Demi chef de rang
   d) Hostess
   e) Kitchen manager
   f) Maitre d'hotel

2. Explain the following styles of service and identify the type of operations likely to use each type:
   a) French Service
   b) Russian Service
   c) American Service

3. Detail the reasons why adequate training is critical to the success of restaurant operations.

4. Evaluate the Foodservice Management Job Analysis presented in the chapter. Identify and defend the three job functions you believe to be most critical.

5. Formula Summary

Food Cost Percentage (including inventory calculations) =

Contribution Margin =

Labor Cost Percentage =

Prime Cost =

Beverage Cost Percentage =

Average Guest Check =

III. Study Questions

Fill in the Blanks

1. Restaurant operations are divided between the _____ and _____.

2. Waitstaff are usually assigned a maximum of _____ tables per station.

3. If a menu item is "86'd" it means that _____.

4. _____ and _____ are needed to forecast restaurant sales.

5. In addition to projecting sales, forecasts are also used to predict _____.

6. One of the advantages of American Service is that the _____ can control plate presentation.

7. The _____ is considered to be the backbone of any restaurant operation.

8. The _____ is the most important part of the kitchen layout.

9. The first step in planning kitchen production is the completion of the _____.

10. _____ should be changed weekly to account for sales trends.

11. The purpose of _____ is to ensure the quality, quantity, and price of items ordered by the restaurant.

12. Budgeting costs fall into two categories: _____ and _____.

13. _____ fluctuate with business levels, whereas _____ remain stable over time.

14. In order to run a business efficiently and effectively, the _____, _____, and _____ of the operation must be considered.

15. Restaurant forecasting is done by taking into consideration _____, _____, _____, and _____.

16. List TGI Friday's five rules for kitchen control.
    a) _____
    b) _____
    c) _____
    d) _____
    e) _____

True/False

1. _____ The income statement compares the liabilities and assets of the operation at a given point in time.

2. _____ Liquidity means that the beverage cost percentage falls within industry norms.

3. _____ From the operations management perspective, the operating or income statement is the most important financial document.

4. _____ Restaurant managers use operating ratios to evaluate the success of the operations they manage.

5. _____ Upscale restaurants maintain a labor cost percentage of from 16% to 18%.

6. _____ Prime costs are comprised of food and beverage costs.

7. _____ Lease costs should not exceed 8% of total sales.

8. _____ The largest single controllable expense is payroll.

9. _____ It is not necessary to have a recipe specification for easy to prepare menu items.

10. _____ Front-of-the-house managers should not involve themselves in back-of-the-house operations.

11. _____ Quick service restaurants have higher payroll costs because of their limited menu and limited service.

Short Answer

1. Explain how the Host/ Hostess contributes to efficient restaurant operations.

_____

_____

_____

_____

_____

2. Explain the difference between "suggestive selling" and "upselling." Provide two examples of each.

_____

_____

_____

_____

_____

_____

_____

_____

3. Compare and contrast formal and informal methods of purchasing. Explain the importance of each major step in the process.

_____

_____

_____

_____

_____

_____

_____

_____

Chapter Eight: Managed Services

After reading and studying Chapter Eight, you should be able to do the following:

1. Outline the different non-commercial food service segments.
2. Describe the five factors that distinguish non-commercial food service operations from commercial ones.
3. Explain the need for and trends in elementary and secondary school food service.
4. Describe the complexities in college and university food service.
5. Identify characteristics and trends in health care and business and industry, and leisure and recreation food service.

The following exercises have been designed to enhance your understanding of the chapter and to assist your studying. These exercises will be most effective if attempted **after** reading the chapter. In addition, space has been provided for you to add terms, notes, and concepts that your instructor may have introduced.

I. Key Words and Concepts

Key Word or Concept	Explanation
1. Batch cooking	
2. Business and Industry Managed Services	
3. Central commissary	
4. Colleges and University Food Service	
5. Commercial foodservice	
6. Daily rate	
7. Dietary guidelines	
8. Direct vendor delivery	
9. Elementary and secondary schools	
10. Food service contractors	
11. Full service cafeteria	
12. Health care managed services	
13. In-flight meal service	

14. Leisure and recreation food service	
15. Liaison personnel	
16. Limited service cafeteria	
17. Managed services	
18. Military food service	
19. Mobile food service	
20. National school lunch program	
21. Nutrition education programs	
22. On-campus dining	
23. Scatter system	
24. Straight line system	
25. Type A menu	
26. Tray line	
27.	
28.	
29.	
30.	

II. Chapter Reflection

1. List the segments of the managed service industry.

2. Considering the features of managed services operations discussed in the chapter, author your own definition for this segment of the hospitality industry.

3. What are the challenges faced by Managed Service Operators within college and university operations?

4. Summarize the roles and responsibilities of food service managers within managed service operations.

5. Identify the unique consideration for managed service operations within health care facilities.

6. Formula Summary

Daily Rate =

III. Study Questions

Fill in the Blanks

1. The cost of the average in-flight meal is _____.

2. Aircraft may have three categories of service: _____, _____, and _____.

3. _____ is the largest and most important component of managed services.

4. In 1946, the United States Government enacted the _____ _____ in response to malnutrition concerns.

5. Many large school districts prepare meals in _____.

6. It is important that school meal menus consider both _____ and _____, as well as what students like to eat.

7. Fast food restaurants hope to earn _____ loyalty through school-based restaurant units.

57

8. Most campus dining is _____ style and is based on _____ menus.

9. Because on-campus students pay for their meals in advance, _____ and _____ are easier and more predictable.

10. Health care managed services are complex because of the _____ of a delicate clientele.

11. The main focus of hospital food service is _____.

12. Within health care food service, labor costs represent _____ to _____% of operating dollars.

True/False

1. _____ Contractors represent approximately 45% of the business and industry market.

2. _____ While in-flight food service operators may be involved with menu planning, they do not influence in-flight service procedures.

3. _____ International flights tend to have better quality food and beverage service than domestic flights.

4. _____ Officers' clubs may be contracted out to managed services operators.

5. _____ Services provided by managed services companies have eliminated the need for MRE's.

6. _____ School lunch meals are nutritionally sound and low in fat.

7. _____ Nutrition education is a required part of the school lunch program.

8. _____ Technological advances, such as sous-vide and cook-chill methods, have helped managed services operators remain competitive.

9. _____ In the business and industry segment, liaison personnel are responsible for overseeing the managed services contractor.

10. _____ Limited-service cafeterias, fast food service, cart and mobile service, and dining rooms are all examples of foodservice within the business and industry segment.

11. _____ For stadium operations, concession stand sales are the only form of food and beverage revenues that can be realized.

12. _____ Leisure and recreation foodservice operations include aquariums, arenas, state parks, and other venues where large numbers of people gather.

Short Answer

1. Identify and explain the factors that influence the types of foodservice offered within the business and idustry segment.

_____
_____
_____
_____
_____
_____
_____

2. Define each of the following terms:
   a) Contractor   b) Self-operator   c) Liaison personnel

_____
_____
_____
_____
_____
_____
_____

3. Compare and contrast health care food service operations when managed by an independent operator and a contract management specialist.

4. Detail the types of food and beverage services provided in the recreation and leisure segment. Identify unique concerns and considerations that must be addressed.

Chapter Nine: Beverages

After reading and studying Chapter Nine, you should be able to do the following:

1. List the various types of wine and describe the wine-making process.
2. Suggest appropriate pairing of wine with foods.
3. List the major wine-growing regions of the world.
4. Distinguish the various types of beer.
5. List the types of spirits and how they are made.
6. Outline the history of coffee and other nonalcoholic beverages.
7. Understand bar and beverage management
8. Explain a restaurant's liability in terms of serving alcoholic beverages.

The following exercises have been designed to enhance your understanding of the chapter and to assist your studying. These exercises will be most effective if attempted **after** reading the chapter. In addition, space has been provided for you to add terms, notes, and concepts that your instructor may have introduced.

I. Key Words and Concepts

Key Word or Concept	Explanation
1. Alcoholic beverage	
2. Beer, malt, hops, and yeast	
3. Champagne	
4. Clarify	
5. Dram shop legislation	
6. Fermentation	
7. Fining	
8. Fortified wines	
9. Inventory control	
10. Mashing	
11. Microbreweries	
12. Must	
13. Non-alcoholic beverage	
14. Prohibition	
15. Proof	

16. Sparkling wines	
17. Spirits (liquor)	
18. TIPS	
19. Vintage	
20. White Spirits	
21. Wines	
22. Wort	
23.	
24.	

II. Chapter Reflection

1. Explain the process of making wine.

2. Explain the brewing process used when making beer.

3. Detail the current trends affecting the non-alcoholic beverage market.

4. Summarize the hospitality industry's response to liquor liability issues.

III. Study Questions

Fill in the Blanks

1. Beverages are categorized into two main groups: _____ and _____.
2. In the United States, wines are named for _____, whereas many European wines are named for _____.
3. _____ and _____ are aromatic wines.
4. _____ wines are usually aged longer than _____ wines.
5. The _____ region produces the best wines in California.
6. _____ is brewed from water, malt, yeast, and hops.
7. _____ is equal to twice the percentage of alcohol in the beverage.
8. A spirit is a liquid that has been _____ and _____.
9. Most _____ comes from the Caribbean Islands, Puerto Rico, and Jamaica.
10. _____ is considered to be the best brandy in the world.
11. _____ are drinks made by mixing two or more ingredients together to create a flavorful beverage.
12. Coffee first came from _____ and _____.
13. _____ produces more than 30% of the world's coffee.
14. _____ is made by adding steamed hot milk to espresso.
15. A bar is divided into _____ where drinks are filled.
16. _____ package is the least expensive pouring brand, while the _____ package is more expensive and are usually asked for by name.
17. _____ usually charge an entrance fee and more per drink than other bars.
18. Whereas _____ generally have very high start-up cost, the profits that can be earned can result in a tremendous return on investment.

19. _____ are based on the model of Italian bars.

20. List the main European wine-producing countries:

   a)_____
   b)_____
   c)_____
   d)_____
   e)_____

True/False

1. _____ Sports bars have experienced a decline in popularity in recent years.

2. _____ Owners of bars are not liable if an employee serves a minor only one alcoholic beverage.

3. _____ Wine can be made from cherries or blackberries.

4. _____ Extra dry champagne is drier in flavor than Brut champagne.

5. _____ Aromatic wines may be flavored with herbs, roots, and flowers.

6. _____ Wine is only aged in stainless steel casks.

7. _____ Whiskey was first made in Canada.

8. _____ Scotch became popular in the United States during Prohibition.

9. _____ Non-alcoholic beers are 100% alcohol free.

10. _____ When compared by weight, tea leaves have more caffeine than coffee beans.

Matching

1. _____ Lager   a) dark in color with strong sweet, strong mild flavor

2. _____ Ale   b) full bodied, somewhat bitter

3. _____ Stout   c) clear, light, and refreshing

4. _____ Pilsner   d) not really a beer, brewed in the Bohemian style

Short Answer

1. Identify and explain the objectives and necessary procedures of a beverage management system.

2. Summarize the key principles involved in matching wine and food.

3. Explain the "lettering" system used to designate the age and quality of cognac blends.

4. List the factors that contribute to the making of a quality cocktail.

Chapter Ten: Recreation and Leisure

After reading and studying Chapter Ten, you should be able to do the following:

1. Discuss the relationship of recreation and leisure to wellness.
2. Explain the origins and extent of government-sponsored recreation.
3. Distinguish between commercial and non-commercial recreation.
4. Name and describe various types of recreation clubs.

The following exercises have been designed to enhance your understanding of the chapter and to assist your studying. These exercises will be most effective if attempted **after** reading the chapter. In addition, space has been provided for you to add terms, notes, and concepts that your instructor may have introduced.

I. Key Words and Concepts

Key Word or Concept	Explanation
1. City clubs	
2. Club management	
3. Commercial recreation	
4. Country club	
5. Government-sponsored recreation	
6. Leisure	
7. National parks	
8. National Parks Service	
9. Non-commercial recreation	
10. Private club	
11. Recreation	
12. Recreation for special populations	
13. Recreation management	
14. Theme parks	
15. Transient occupancy taxes	
16. Voluntary organizations	

17. Wellness	
18.	
19.	
20.	

II. Chapter Reflection

1. Explain the reasons why recreation is an integral part of society and culture.

2. Detail the role of government in the development of recreation and leisure services.

3. Summarize the professional guidelines for club managers as established by the Club Manager's Association of America.

4. Describe the policy and legal issues considered by recreation professionals.

III. Study Questions

Fill in the Blanks

1. _____ is best described as time free from work.
2. The National Parks Service was founded in _____ by Congress.
3. Canada has _____ national parks and more than 20 national historic sites.
4. _____ recreation programming has been planned around themes since the 1950s.
5. _____ came of age in the 1920s and 1930s.

6. _____ can be defined as "recreation for which the consumer pays and for which the supplier expects to make a profit."

7. Theme parks are commonly planned around _____, _____, and/or _____ themes.

8. Private clubs provide a place for members to gather for _____, _____, _____, or _____ reasons.

9. Club management is similar to _____ management.

10. The internal management of private clubs is governed by a _____ and _____.

11. Country clubs have two types of membership: _____ and _____.

12. _____ are non-governmental, nonprofit agencies that serve the public-at-large or a specific segment of the population.

True/False

1. _____ Campus recreation programs are limited to the coordination of intramural and competitive sports events.

2. _____ The Department of Defense sponsors recreation activities through Moral, Welfare, and Recreation (MWR) programs.

3. _____ Business and industry support employee recreation programs because studies have shown that employees who participate in the programs are more productive.

4. _____ Therapeutic recreation is another term for massage therapy.

5. _____ Governments raise revenues for recreation programs exclusively from income, sales, and property taxes.

6. _____ Today's private clubs are modeled after clubs that originated in Spain and France.

7. _____ City clubs are predominately sports oriented.

8. _____ Health clubs have more exclusive recreation programs than those programs offered by multipurpose clubs.

9. _____ Country clubs have become more exclusive in recent years as the demand for membership has increased.

10. _____ Theme parks may be single- or multi-themed.

Matching

1. _____ Professional clubs   a) include organizations such as the Veterans of Foreign Wars, Elks, and the Shriners

2. _____ Athletic clubs   b) cater to people in the same occupation, such as the National Press Club and the Lawyer's Club

3. _____ Dining clubs   c) cater to NCOs and enlisted officers, offer recreation, entertainment, and food and beverage

4. _____ Social clubs   d) provide members with the opportunity to work out; may also have lounges, bars, and restaurants

5. _____ Military clubs   e) usually located in large office buildings; memberships usually given away as part of a lease agreement

6. _____ Fraternal clubs   f) provide members with a mooring as well as food and beverage facilities

7. _____ Proprietary clubs   g) give members an opportunity to enjoy each other's company and provide high quality food and beverage

8. _____ Yacht clubs   h) operate on a for-profit basis; often linked to housing developments

Short Answer

1. List and explain the demographic factors that affect participation in recreational activities.

_____

_____

_____

_____

2. Detail the ways in which club management is similar to hotel management.

3. Describe the roles of the following positions in club management:
   President   Vice-president   Secretary
   Treasurer   Committees

4. Define "recreation for special populations" and identify the groups served by this segment of the industry.

Chapter Eleven: The Gaming Entertainment Industry

After reading and studying Chapter Eleven, you should be able to do the following:

1. Outline the history of the gaming entertainment industry.
2. Describe the various activities related to gaming entertainment.
3. Explain how gaming entertainment is converging with other aspects of the hospitality business.
4. Discuss the controversies surrounding the gaming entertainment industry.

The following exercises have been designed to enhance your understanding of the chapter and to assist your studying. These exercises will be most effective if attempted **after** reading the chapter. In addition, space has been provided for you to add terms, notes, and concepts that your instructor may have introduced.

I. Key Words and Concepts

Key Word or Concept	Explanation
1. Baccarat	
2. Bet	
3. Big 6	
4. Blackjack	
5. Casino	
6. Craps	
7. Drop entertainment	
8. Gaming	
9. Gambling	
10. Handle	
11. Indian Gaming Regulatory Act (IGRA)	
12. Poker	
13. Roulette	
14. Social gambler	
15. Wager	

16. Win	
17.	
18.	
19.	
20.	

II. Chapter Reflection

1. Compare and contrast the terms "gaming entertainment" and "gambling."

2. Trace the development of the gaming entertainment industry.

3. Identify the similarities between recent gaming entertainment projects.

III. Study Questions

Fill in the Blanks

1. Gaming entertainment served the customer base of "_____ gamblers."
2. _____ is the net amount of money spent by the customer.
3. Approximately _____ of Americans disapprove of casino entertainment entirely.
4. The total amount wagered or bet is referred to as the _____.
5. _____ and _____ make up about 85% of consumer spending in the gaming industry.
6. _____ is the second most popular vacation destination in the United States.
7. State-run _____ were established in the 1960s.
8. Gaming is considered to be a _____ industry.
9. Casino gaming was legalized in New Jersey with the passing of _____.
10. For every _____ dollars in revenue, the casino industry created _____ direct jobs.

11. Beginning in the 1970s, casino ownership has shifted from individuals to _____.

12. _____ is one of the most tightly regulated industries in the United States.

13. Gaming entertainment hotel properties are generally _____ than non-gaming properties.

14. The _____ is usually a separate division within gaming entertainment operations and does not fall under hotel operations.

True/ False

1. _____ Food and beverage outlets within gaming entertainment facilities specialize in high quality food and service.

2. _____ Riverboat casinos were first legalized in Illinois.

3. _____ Charitable games are not considered to be part of the gaming industry.

4. _____ Casino players tend to be highly educated and hold white collar jobs.

5. _____ The average bet by table game players is 75 dollars.

6. _____ The Nevada Gaming Commission established strict rules determining who could be licensed to operate gaming operations.

7. _____ The gaming entertainment industry is an evolution of the casino industry.

8. _____ Native American tribes are required to pay a 23% tax on all gaming revenues to the state in which they conduct business.

9. _____ Gaming entertainment operations have no impact on crime statistics.

10. _____ Mirage resorts operate primarily in Atlantic City.

Short Answer

1. Identify the provision of the Indian Gaming Regulation Act (IGRA).

2. List and describe the unique aspects of the key players within the gaming entertainment industry.

3. Detail the career opportunities available in the gaming entertainment industry.

Chapter Twelve: Meetings, Conventions, and Expositions

After reading and studying Chapter Twelve, you should be able to do the following:

1. Name the main hospitality industry associations.
2. Describe the various types of meetings.
3. Explain the differences among meetings, expositions, and conventions.
4. Describe the role of the meeting planner.
5. Explain the primary responsibility of a convention and visitors' bureau or authority.
6. List the steps in event management.

The following exercises have been designed to enhance your understanding of the chapter and to assist your studying. These exercises will be most effective if attempted **after** reading the chapter. In addition, space has been provided for you to add terms, notes, and concepts that your instructor may have introduced.

I. Key Words and Concepts

Key Word or Concept	Explanation
1. Associations	
2. Boardroom style	
3. Booking manager	
4. Classroom style	
5. Clinic	
6. Consumer show	
7. Convention	
8. Convention centers	
9. Conventions and Visitors' Bureaus	
10. Event document	
11. Expositions	
12. Familiarization (FAM) trip	
13. Forum	
14. Incentive market	
15. Meeting	

16. Meeting Planner	
17. Off-premise catering	
18. Seminar	
19. Site inspection	
20. SMERF	
21. Special events	
22. Symposium	
23. Theater style	
24. Trade show	
25. Workshop	
26.	
27.	
28.	

II. Chapter Reflection

1. List the reasons meetings are held.

2. Outline the format of a typical convention.

3. Detail the responsibilities of the positions of Meeting Planners and Event Planners.

4. List the factors that should be considered when determining a site for a MICE event.

III. Study Questions

Fill in the Blanks

1. Associations date back to the Middle Ages and originally sought to ensure _____ and _____ for members.

2. _____ allow manufacturers to display equipment and/or goods to attendees at a convention or trade show.

3. The meeting planner is shown all facets of the hotel, food and beverage outlets, and meeting room facilities during the _____.

4. A _____ is a non-profit organization that seeks to solicit business or pleasure-seeking visitors to a community.

5. Convention centers generate revenue from _____ as well as _____, concessions stand rentals, and vending machines.

6. The _____ is usually responsible for booking convention business more than eighteen months in advance.

7. The _____ is responsible for booking the correct space for an event.

8. The _____ defines in writing all of the client's requirements for the upcoming event.

9. The _____ is the key contact between the convention center and the client.

10. The _____ meeting allows convention center staff to discuss the upcoming events at the center and to address any areas of concern.

11. _____ are conferences, workshops, seminars, or other events designed to bring people together to exchange information.

12. The three most common room setups for meetings are _____, _____, and _____.

13. _____ travel is awarded to top performing employees in a company and may be modest or extremely lavish in nature.

14. _____ are annual gatherings of individuals that share a common interest.

15. _____ facet of hospitality focuses on conceiving, designing, developing, and producing ideas.

16. List the five major functions of associations:
    a)_____
    b)_____
    c)_____
    d)_____
    e)_____

17. List five organizations represented by the Convention and Visitors' Bureau:
    a)_____
    b)_____
    c)_____
    d)_____
    e)_____

18. List six services provided by Specialized Services:
    a)_____
    b)_____
    c)_____
    d)_____
    e)_____
    f)_____

19. The primary sources of revenue for MICE events are:
    a)_____
    b)_____
    c)_____

True/False

1. _____ Annual conventions must be held in the same city every year.

2. _____ Convention travelers spend approximately twice as much as vacation travelers each day.

3. _____ Exhibitors are invited to show their products free of charge at annual conventions.

4. _____ Annual conventions provide significant revenues for associations.

5. _____ The majority of conventions are held in hotels and are three to five days in duration.

6. _____ Professional meeting planners are involved in the planning process only until the convention center's staff becomes involved.

7. _____ The Convention and Visitors' Bureau staff acts as a sales team for the city.

8. _____ Convention centers often have subcontractors to handle special meeting needs such as lighting, electrical, and communications.

9. _____ The event profile is based on the event contract.

10. _____ The event document is distributed to convention center staff two weeks prior to the event.

11. _____ On average, MICE tourists spend twice as much as other tourists.

12. _____ The average lead time for planning a meeting is 2 to 3 years.

Short Answer

1. List and define the different forms meetings can take.

_____

_____

_____

_____

_____

2. What are the primary responsibilities of a Convention and Visitors' Bureau?

3. What information about a group should a catering consultant obtain when planning an event? Give examples of how this information might shape the event planning process.

Chapter Thirteen: Marketing, Human Resources, and Culture

After reading and studying Chapter Thirteen, you should be able to do the following:

1. Discuss the importance of environmental scanning as it relates to marketing and sales.
2. List and explain each of the steps in the marketing process.
3. Show how a competitor analysis is conducted.
4. Explain the term *product life cycle*.
5. State the differences between marketing and sales.
6. List and explain the steps in human resources management and development processes.
7. Describe culture and ethnic diversity.

The following exercises have been designed to enhance your understanding of the chapter and to assist your studying. These exercises will be most effective if attempted **after** reading the chapter. In addition, space has been provided for you to add terms, notes, and concepts that your instructor may have introduced.

I. Key Words and Concepts

Key Word or Concept	Explanation
1. Age Discrimination Act	
2. Americans with Disabilities Act	
3. Civil Rights Act	
4. Comparison matrix	
5. Compensation	
6. Competitor analysis	
7. Culture	
8. Demographics	
9. Economic analysis	
10. Employee Assistance Program (EAP)	
11. Employee development	
12. Employee retention	

13. Employee stock ownership plan	
14. Equal Employment Opportunity Commission	
15. Environmental analysis	
16. Equal Pay Act	
17. Ethnic diversity	
18. Exempt and non-exempt employees	
19. Expense accounts	
20. Fair Labor Standards Act	
21. Harassment	
22. Human resource management	
23. Job description	
24. Lifestyles	
25. Market assessment	
26. Market demand	
27. Market share	
28. Marketing action plan	
29. Marketing goals and objectives	
30. Marketing mix	
31. Orientation	
32. Performance appraisal	
33. Performance evaluation	
34. Productivity standards	
35. Product life cycle	
36. Recruitment	
37. Selection	
38. Target markets	

39. Task analysis	
40. Training	
41.	
42.	
43.	
44.	
45.	

II. Chapter Reflection

1. Summarize the 11 characteristics of marketing orientation.

2. Explain the significance of the following aspects of environmental analysis:
    a) economic impacts
    b) social analysis
    c) political analysis
    d) technological analysis

3. Define "Pertinent Ps" that comprise the marketing mix.

4. Outline the key functions of human resource management.

III. Study Questions

Fill in the Blanks

1. _____ seeks to determine what guests desire and to provide it at a reasonable cost and profit.
2. Marketing begins with _____ and _____.
3. _____ provides information regarding the economic, political, social, and technological influences that could affect the hospitality industry.
4. _____ provide information regarding society within a particular area.
5. _____ seeks to determine if there is a need for a product or service in the market and determine its potential.
6. _____ assists a company with identifying the competition's strengths and weaknesses.
7. _____ are "how-to" tactics that are used to meet goals.
8. All products and services go through a predictable _____.
9. Prices may be determined in two main ways: _____ and _____.
10. _____ is paid, non-personal communication control by the organization whereas _____ is not paid for and is not controlled by the organization.
11. _____ are designed to entice consumers to purchase goods or services.
12. A _____ is formed when two or more hospitality/ tourism organizations come together to create an overall marketing campaign.
13. _____ provides companies with information to determine the effectiveness of a marketing strategy.
14. About _____ of a hotel's business is generated by _____ of its guests.

15. _____ seeks to determine how each element of a job impacts the experience of the guest.

16. _____ and _____ are two key elements in the process of finding the most suitable employee for an available position.

17. Attendance at an _____ session is usually required for all new employees.

18. Compensation includes not only the amount of wages or salaries paid to an employee, but also _____.

19. List the five different types of pre-employment tests.

   a)_____
   b)_____
   c)_____
   d)_____
   e)_____

20. List and briefly describe the three common distortions of performance appraisals.

   a)_____
   _____
   b)_____
   _____
   c)_____
   _____

True/False

1. _____ Exempt employees are exempted from working overtime hours unless they are paid time and a half their hourly wage.

2. _____ The Age Discrimination Act prevents companies from making employment decisions on the basis of age.

3. _____ The American with Disabilities Act requires that companies make "readily achievable" modifications to assist disabled employees.

4. _____ Culture is learned behavior that influences the way that people behave.

5. _____ Labor is the single highest cost in the hospitality industry.

6. _____ A comparison matrix allows a company to determine the popularity of the various products they offer.

7. _____ Price is the most visible aspect of the Marketing Mix.

8. _____ Public relations seek to build a positive image of the organization.

9. _____ The job description is a general outline of a position's requirements.

10. _____ Productivity standards are an important tool used in controlling labor costs.

Short Answer

1. Explain the difference between the terms "sales" and "marketing."

_____

_____

_____

_____

2. Define the following forms of training:
   - a) apprentice
   - b) simulation
   - c) certification
   - d) on-the-job
   - e) off-the-job

_____

_____

_____

_____

_____

_____

3. Detail the issues related to conducting employee performance appraisals.

4. Explain how multiculturalism and ethnic diversity impact the hospitality/ tourism workplace.

Chapter Fourteen: Leadership and Management

After reading and studying Chapter Fourteen, you should be able to do the following:

1. Distinguish the characteristics and attributes of leaders.
2. Define leadership.
3. Distinguish between transactional and transformational leadership.
4. Differentiate between leadership and management.
5. Describe the key management functions.
6. Define ethics and apply the importance of ethical behaviors to the hospitality industry.

The following exercises have been designed to enhance your understanding of the chapter and to assist your studying. These exercises will be most effective if attempted **after** reading the chapter. In addition, space has been provided for you to add terms, notes, and concepts that your instructor may have introduced.

I. Key Words and Concepts

Key Word or Concept	Explanation
1. Centralized company	
2. Communicating	
3. Controlling	
4. Decentralized company	
5. Decision making	
6. Equity theory	
7. Ethics	
8. Expectancy theory	
9. Forecasting	
10. Goal-setting theory	
11. Herzberg's motivation and hygiene factors	
12. Leadership	
13. Management	
14. Maslow's hierarchy of needs	

15. Motivating	
16. Organizing	
17. Planning	
18. Process theory	
19. Span of control	
20. Transactional leadership	
21. Transformational leadership	
22.	
23.	
24.	
25.	

II. Chapter Reflection

1. Identify and explain the practices common to effective leaders.

2. Differentiate between transactional leadership and transformational leadership.

3. Compare and contrast the terms "management" and "leadership."

4. List and explain the seven steps involved in organizational planning.

5. Outline the eight major steps involved in the decision making process.

6. Detail the influence of ethics upon practices in the hospitality industry.

III. Study Questions

Fill in the Blanks

1. Transformational leadership involves three major factors: _____, _____, and _____.

2. _____ is a formal process through which objective are met through the efforts of subordinates, whereas _____ is the influencing the behavior of others in a desired way.

3. _____ help top managers plan for the entire corporation while considering the interdependence of individual departments.

4. Managers need _____ to assist them with understanding techniques, methods, and procedures involved in operations.

5. The _____ or "shadow" organization develops as people interact with one another on the job.

6. Centralized decisions are made at the _____ level.

7. Today, the accepted span of control for managers is _____ employees.

8. Program decisions generally become _____.

9. _____ are usually made in response to unforeseen events.

10. Communication requires a _____, a message, and a _____.

11. The informal communication channel in an organization is referred to as the _____.

12. Identify three benefits gained by communicating with staff informally.
    a) _____
    b) _____
    c) _____

13. List the three benefits of management function of control.

   a)_____

   b)_____

   c)_____

True/False

1. _____ Technical skills become more important the higher a manager rises on the corporate ladder.

2. _____ Social responsibility requires community involvement as well as responsible business practices.

3. _____ Ethics are based solely on one's own value system.

4. _____ The Equity Theory of Motivation is based on the premise that people will put forth effort equivalent to the perceived reward.

5. _____ Content Motivation Theory asserts that several factors influence a person whether or not to do something.

6. _____ Face to face tends to be the best form of communication.

7. _____ The more sophisticated a company is, the fewer programmed decisions will be made because of the intensive training employees have received.

8. _____ Successful organizations are able to share their corporate philosophies with both employees and guests.

Matching

1. _____ Forecasting — a) may be formal or informal; serves as "the oil that lubricates" all other management functions

2. _____ Planning — b) the process of arranging resources of the organization so that activities efficiently contribute to the organization's goals

3. _____ Organizing — c) may be centralized or decentralized, programmed or non-programmed; should be done in consideration of the organization's goals

4. _____ Decision making — d) accuracy is very important because in the hospitality industry goods and services are perishable; used to predict the level of business volume

5. _____ Communicating — e) the art or process of initiating or sustaining behavior toward established goals

6. _____ Motivating — f) may be strategic or tactical; the purpose is to help the organization move toward established goals

7. _____ Controlling — g) provides information for management to make decisions, and helps detect whether or not the organization has met its goals

Short Answer

1. Identify ways to be a hospitality leader rather than a hospitality manager.

_____
_____
_____
_____
_____
_____

2. Explain the elements of effective communication.

3. Explain the following motivation theories:
   a) intrinsic and extrinsic theories
   b) vicarious theories
   c) content theories
   d) process theories
   e) goal setting theories

Answer Key

In this section you will find the answers to **Fill-in-the-Blanks, True/ False,** and **Matching** questions from each chapter. Please refer to the Glossary section of your textbook for assistance with the **Keywords and Concepts** sections. For the **Chapter Review** and **Short Answer** sections, the text pages have been provided for your reference.

Chapter One:
Chapter Reflection
1. pages 11-12; 17; 12; 19; 20; 22; 23-28
2. pages 5-9
3. page 21
4. page 18

Study Questions

Fill in the blanks
1. pineapple
2. tourism
3. managed services
4. knowledge, skills, and abilities
5. Malcolm Baldrige Award; Ritz-Carlton
6. moment of truth
7. ladies and gentlemen; ladies and gentlemen
8. peer interview; interact successfully with guests
9. internships
10. academic record, work experience, and extracurricular activities
11. thank you note
12. state the purpose, involve all employees, monitor, update, and follow.

True/ False
1. True
2. True
3. False
4. False
5. True
6. False
7. False
8. True

Matching
1. b
2. c
3. d
4. e
5. a

Short Answer
1. page 9
2. pages 14
3. pages 14-16
4. pages 33-34

Chapter Two:
Chapter Reflection
1. pages 40-41
2. page 41
3. pages 42-57
4. pages 57-60
5. pages 62-64

Study Questions

Fill in the blanks
1. Egypt; Britain
2. Amtrak
3. Retrenchment of major carriers, new airlines, lower fares, mega carriers
4. City-level offices of Tourism
5. Certified Travel Counselor (CTC)
6. the U.S. has higher labor costs, prohibit on-board casinos, higher construction costs.
7. independent tour wholesalers, airlines, retail travel agents
8. physical, cultural, interpersonal, status, and prestige

True/ False
1. True
2. False
3. True
4. False
5. True
6. False
7. False
8. True
9. True
10. True
11. True
12. True

Matching
1. i
2. g
3. e
4. b
5. d
6. h
7. c
8. a
9. f

Short Answer
1. pages 46-47
2. pages 51-57
3. page 64
4. page 72
5. pages 79-83
6. pages 60-61

Chapter Three:
Chapter Reflection
1. pages 96-98
2. pages 113-115
3. pages 120-127
4. pages 102-104

Study Questions

Fill in the blanks
1. Transportation
2. Automobiles
3. 3%; 4%
4. the cyclical nature of demand; the high degree of capital investment
5. Patriot; Starwood
6. First mortgage loans
7. captured

True/False
1. False
2. True
3. False
4. False
5. True
6. True
7. False
8. True
9. True
10. True

Matching
1. b
2. g
3. a
4. h
5. d
6. c
7. e
8. i
9. f

Short Answer
1. pages 98-101
2. page 108
3. pages 112
4. pages 118-120

Chapter Four:
Chapter Reflection
1. pages 153-155; 158-170; 176-192
2. pages 153-155
3. pages 163-165

Study Questions
Fill in the blanks
1. provide lodging accommodations
2. serve society; make a profit
3. upselling; yield management
4. demand; supply
5. city ledger
6. lodging central reservation systems; airlines
7. profit analysis by segment
8. person hours per occupied room
9. return on investment, satisfied guests, happy employees
10. reservations management, rooms management, guest account management, general management

True/ False
1.	True	6.	False
2.	False	7.	True
3.	True	8.	False
4.	False	9.	False
5.	False	10.	True

Matching
1.	c	5.	a
2.	e	6.	b
3.	g	7.	d
4.	f		

Short Answer
1. page 157
2. page 177
3. pages 177-178
4. pages 193-194

Chapter Five:
Chapter Reflection
1. pages 204-217; 222-226; 230
2. pages 217-221
3. page 225
4. pages 228-230

Study Questions
Fill in the blanks
1. General manager
2. 20%
3. 12th; 15th
4. ratios
5. brigade; Escoffier
6. 16%; 24%
7. Chief steward
8. Banquet; catering
9. catering event order; banquet event order
10. telephone; door knob hangers
11. meetings, conventions, dinners, luncheons, weddings
12. vending machines on guests' floors, timely scheduling, well-trained staff, technology

True/ False
1.	False	6.	True
2.	True	7.	True
3.	True	8.	False
4.	False	9.	False
5.	False	10.	True

Matching
1. c
2. d
3. a
4. b

Short Answer
1. pages 206-207
2. pages 217-218
3. page 219
4. pages 220-221
5. page 226

Chapter Six:
Chapter Reflection
1. pages 243-247
2. page 250
3. pages 266-284
4. pages 255-257
5. pages 259-263

Study Questions
Fill in the blanks
1. niche
2. catchment area
3. 500
4. 6 to 8; 2 to 4; 8 to 16; 4 to 6
5. Equipment capacity and layout
6. Chinese restaurants
7. Comparative; item cost
8. Food cost percentage; contribution margin; sales volume
9. Accuracy in menu laws
10. readily available; adaptable
11. expense account; special occasion
12. a la carte, table d'hôte, du jour, California, cyclical
13. (see full list page 250)

True/ False
1. False
2. False
3. False
4. True
5. True
6. True
7. True
8. False
9. True
10. False

Short Answer
1. pages 285-287
2. page 268
3. page 261
4. pages 247-249

Chapter Seven:
Chapter Reflection
1. pages 298-301; 303; 308
2. page 303-307
3. page 302-303
4. page 327-330

Study Questions
Fill in the blanks
1. Front of the house; back of the house
2. five
3. it is not available
4. guest count; average guest check amount
5. staff levels needed
6. chef
7. back of the house
8. cooking line
9. production sheet
10. par levels
11. product specification
12. fixed; variable
13. variable costs; fixed costs
14. mission; goals; objectives
15. meal period, day of week, special holiday, previous forecast
16. order it well, receive it well, store it well, make it to recipe, don't let it die in the window

True/ False
1. False	5. False	9. False
2. False	6. False	10. False
3. True	7. True	11. False
4. True	8. True	

Short Answer
1. page 300
2. pages 3020-303
3. page 314

Chapter Eight:
Chapter Reflection
1. page 338
2. page 338
3. pages 348-351
4. pages 351-356
5. pages 358-361

Study Questions
Fill in the blanks
1. six dollars
2. coach; business class ; first class
3. military food service
4. National School Lunch Act
5. commissaries
6. cost; good nutrition
7. brand
8. cafeteria; cycle
9. budget; guest count forecasts
10. diverse needs
11. trayline
12. 55%; 66%

True/ False
1. True
2. True
3. True
4. True
5. False
6. False
7. True
8. True
9. True
10. True
11. False
12. True

Short Answer
1. pages 361-362
2. page 361
3. pages 360-361
4. pages 363-365

Chapter Nine:
Chapter Reflection
1. pages 375-376
2. page 382
3. pages 390-394
4. pages 401-403

Study Questions

Fill in the blanks
1. alcoholic; non-alcoholic
2. grape type; region of origin
3. vermouth; aperitifs
4. Red; white
5. North and central coastal
6. Beer
7. Proof
8. fermented; distilled
9. rum
10. Cognac
11. Cocktail
12. Ethiopia; Mocha
13. Brazil
14. Cappuccino
15. stations
16. Well; call
17. Nightclubs
18. Microbreweries
19. Coffeehouses
20. Germany, Italy, Spain, Portugal, France

True/False
1. False
2. False
3. True
4. False
5. True
6. False
7. False
8. False
9. False
10. True

Matching
1. c
2. b
3. a
4. d

Short Answer
1. pages 394 -397
2. pages 376-377
3. pages 388-389
4. page 389

Chapter Ten:
Chapter Reflection
1. pages 410-411
2. pages 411-416
3. pages 421-422
4. pages 412-413

Study Questions

Fill in the blanks
1. Recreation
2. 1916
3. 29
4. Canadian
5. Recreation management
6. Commercial recreation
7. historical; cultural; geographical
8. social; professional; fraternal
9. hotel
10. constitution; by-laws
11. full; social
12. Voluntary

True/ False
1.	False	6.	False
2.	True	7.	False
3.	True	8.	False
4.	False	9.	False
5.	False	10.	True

Matching
1.	b	5.	c
2.	d	6.	a
3.	e	7.	h
4.	g	8.	f

Short Answer
1. page 412
2. page 421
3. pages 422-423
4. page 431

Chapter Eleven:
Chapter Reflection
1. pages 438-442
2. pages 442-446
3. pages 454-460

Study Questions

Fill in the blanks
1. social
2. Win
3. 8%
4. handle
5. Lotteries; casinos
6. Las Vegas
7. lotteries
8. privileged
9. Casino Control Act
10. $1 million; 13
11. publicly held corporations
12. Casino entertainment
13. larger
14. Food and beverage department

True/ False
1.	True	6.	True
2.	False	7.	True
3.	False	8.	False
4.	True	9.	False
5.	False	10.	False

Short Answer
1. pages 444-445
2. pages 450-454
3. pages 461-463

Chapter Twelve:
Chapter Reflection
1. page 477
2. page 473
3. page 484
4. page 476

Study Questions
Fill in the blanks
1. proper wages; working conditions
2. Expositions
3. site inspection
4. convention and visitors' bureau
5. space rental; food and beverage sales
6. Convention and visitor's bureau
7. booking manager
8. event profile
9. event manager
10. Week at a Glance (WAG)
11. Meetings
12. theater style; classroom; boardroom
13. Incentive
14. Conventions
15. Special events
16. governmental/ political voice, marketing avenues, education, member services, networking
17. transportation, hotels and motels, restaurants, attractions, suppliers
18. transportation, entertainment, audiovisual, escorts and tour guides, convention set-up, and destination management
19. Attendee registration fees, exhibition space rental, sponsorship, program advertising

True/ False
1. False
2. True
3. False
4. True
5. False
6. False
7. True
8. True
9. False
10. False
11. True
12. False

Short Answer
1. page 471
2. pages 485-486
3. page 480

Chapter Thirteen:
Chapter Reflection
1. pages 506-507
2. pages 507-510
3. pages 513-515
4. pages 519-531

Study Questions

Fill in the blanks
1. Marketing
2. corporate philosophy; mission
3. Environment Analysis
4. Demographics
5. Market assessment
6. Competitor analysis
7. Objectives
8. life cycle
9. comparative; cost plus approach
10. Advertising; publicity
11. Sales promotion
12. partnership
13. Performance evaluation
14. 80%; 20%
15. Task analysis
16. Recruitment; selection
17. orientation program
18. benefits
19. personality, attitude, skill, psychological, drug screening
20. recent behavior influence, halo effect, like-me

True/ False
1. False
2. False
3. True
4. True
5. True
6. False
7. False
8. True
9. False
10. True

Short Answer
1. pages 506-507 and 516-518
2. page 523
3. pages 524-526
4. pages 532-534

Chapter Fourteen:
Chapter Reflection
1. pages 542 and 546-552
2. pages 543-545
3. pages 552-556
4. page 559
5. page 561
6. pages 570-573

Study Questions
Fill in the blanks
1. charisma; individual consideration; intellectual stimulation
2. Management; leadership
3. Conceptual skills
4. technical skills
5. informal
6. corporate
7. 12
8. standard operating procedures (SOPs)
9. Non-programmed decisions
10. sender; receiver
11. grapevine
12. identify potential problems, gain staff commitment, gather information
13. establish standards of performance, measure current performance act on performance variances.

True/ False
1.	False	4.	False	7.	False
2.	True	5.	True	8.	True
3.	False	6.	True		

Matching
1.	d	4.	c	6.	e
2.	f	5.	a	7.	g
3.	b				

Short Answer
1. pages 553-554
2. pages 564-566
3. pages 567-570